Homesteaders in Nebraska

by Horatio Treemont
illustrated by Philomena O'Neill

PEARSON

Scott
Foresman

Editorial Offices: Glenview, Illinois • Parsippany, New Jersey • New York, New York
Sales Offices: Needham, Massachusetts • Duluth, Georgia • Glenview, Illinois
Coppell, Texas • Ontario, California • Mesa, Arizona

Chapter One

I was only 10 years old when my family moved away from the crowded city of Philadelphia out to the sprawling prairies of Nebraska.

It was not a move I had expected to make. After all, Philadelphia had been my home all my life. The idea of moving to a strange, desolate part of the country roused a queasy feeling deep in the pit of my stomach.

What was "Nebraska," anyway? What was a "prairie"? Why would anyone want to abandon the comforts of big city life in favor of such a strange, uncertain, and Spartan existence?

Why, indeed?

"I'm sorry, Timothy," my father said on a spring night in 1880. "But we've got to go."

"There's no more work for your father here," said my mother, stroking his hand.

I understood. Although he had never earned a lot of money, my father always made enough to keep us comfortable. We lived in a small apartment. We dined on cabbage, potatoes, and the occasional few shavings of meat, and we wore the cheapest clothes.

Nonetheless, we were happy. We had one another and the familiar trappings of our daily routine could be quite comforting. School in the morning and afternoon, chores later in the day, supper and homework in the evening, then lights out, a full night's sleep, and the cycle began anew. It was hardly exhilarating, but it was the only life I'd ever known.

"What's in Nebraska?" I asked.

"The government set up a program called the Homestead Act about two decades ago," said my father. "Have you heard of it, Timothy?"

"No, sir," I said. I looked at my six-year-old sister, Scarlet. Usually she claimed to know everything, but now she sat quietly, listening for once.

"Well," said my father, "this is how it works. The government wants people to move out West."

"Why?" asked Scarlet.

"There's a lot of overcrowding in the cities here in the East. There's also a lot of land just going to waste out West," he said.

"How does that affect us?" I asked.

"Here's the deal," said my father. "Under the provisions of the Homestead Act, we can go to Nebraska and claim 160 acres of land."

"Is that a lot?" I asked.

"It's about one-quarter of a square mile," said my father. "It's a nice-sized piece of land."

"And the government is going to just give the land to us?" I asked, suspiciously. "For free?"

"Not exactly for free," my father admitted. "We'll have to pay a small registration fee, right off the bat. But after that . . . well, the government lets us have the land for five years. We won't own it, but we'll be allowed to use it, as we see fit."

"We're going to grow crops," said my mother, smiling. "Imagine that, children! Our own garden, bursting with fresh fruits and vegetables. And animals! We'll raise some chickens, and maybe a cow or two."

"Doggies!" shouted my sister, who had always longed for a puppy of her own. "Can we have doggies, Mommy?"

"Well, perhaps we can have a dog," said my mother. "If Daddy doesn't mind."

"We'll see, Scarlet " said my father, unwilling to make any promises. "I'm not saying yes, and I'm not saying no. We'll see how things play out."

"What happens when the five years are over?" I asked my father.

"A government man will check up on us," he said. "He'll see if we've built a home and made improvements to the commissioned land."

"Improvements?" I asked. "What does that mean?"

"He'll look to see if we've planted crops, or dug irrigation ditches, or put up a fence. Things like that. If he feels that we've improved the land, it'll be ours to keep. Free and clear."

"Really?" I asked, surprised.

"We won't have to pay," said my mother, nodding and smiling.

"I know it'll be tough at first," my father admitted. "But think about it! Our own land, with our own house sitting on it! We'll be self-sufficient too. No more worrying about finding work. Your mother and I will be our own bosses!"

When my mother came to say goodnight later that evening, she sensed my mood. "Won't it be grand, Timmy?" she asked. "A place of our own?"

"Yes," I admitted. "But what about all the things we'll leave behind? I won't be able to see Tony anymore, or Morris, or Danny."

My mother smiled a little sadly. "That's true," she said, "but you'll make new friends in Nebraska. You can write your friends back here and tell them about your new life."

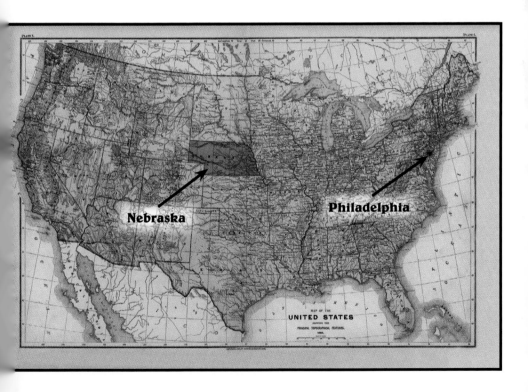

"What's it like in Nebraska, Ma?" I asked abruptly. "What are the schools like? What's it like working on a farm? What's it like living on a prairie? Are there trees? Or is everything flat, like a sheet of paper?"

My mother smiled and shrugged.

"Timmy, the truth is that I don't know."

"But aren't you scared?" I asked.

"Sure," she said. "It's natural to fear change. But change is also exciting! We'll be pioneers in a new land. Who knows what adventures we'll have?"

Chapter Two

A few months later, we had moved to our new home, a sleepy little settlement called Burgess, located deep in the heart of Nebraska.

It was a settlement only in the loosest sense of the word. Our nearest neighbor was a good five miles away, down a rough and dusty dirt road. I don't imagine that there were more than twenty families living there, within a fifty-mile radius.

Nebraska was every bit as desolate as I had imagined—perhaps even more so. Everything was flat. As far as the eye could see, vast empty prairies sprawled out to the horizon. I didn't hate my new home. But it certainly was not a case of love at first sight.

"There's nothing here," said Scarlet, more than a little disappointed. "Just dirt and grass."

"There's nothing here *yet*," said my father, with forced cheerfulness. "But we're going to change that, children."

"Where will we live?" I asked.

"We're going to build our own home," said my father, with a grim sort of confidence.

"But how?" I asked, dubiously. "I don't see any trees. Where will we get the timber?"

"We're going to build what people around here call a 'soddy,'" he explained.

"A soddy," repeated Scarlet. "What's that?"

"Well," my father explained, "it's an earthen house made out of grass and dirt."

"Grass and dirt!" Scarlet and I said in unison. We were both astounded and a little disgusted.

"We'll dig up blocks of the prairie turf," my father explained. "The sod is anchored in place by tough, durable roots. They'll act like twine to bind our sod blocks together."

"Then, we'll build a house out of the blocks," said my mother. "We'll just stack them up."

"When we're done," my father continued, "we'll build a roof of wood and cover it over with more sod to make it really secure."

The idea of building an entire house out of sod was intriguing, I'll admit. But I did have one question. "What happens when it rains?" I asked.

"Soddies are supposed to be *fairly* durable," said my father unconvincingly. "So I don't think we have to worry too much."

"When will we make the soddy?" asked Scarlet. "I wanna see a soddy!"

To my surprise, Scarlet seemed to find the prospect of living in a dirt house to be very exciting.

"We'll start tonight," my parents said.

We did begin building our soddy that evening. It was harder work than I had ever done, but that's not saying much. Until that day, the hardest work I'd ever done was watering my mother's flowers or making my bed.

This work was different. Of course, my parents did the hardest part, but Scarlet and I pitched in and helped. No doubt about it, they were grateful for the extra hands.

The funny thing was, we wanted to help. It made us feel strong and grown-up. We felt like real pioneers, as we slowly got covered with dirt, and our arms and legs began to ache. How many kids back East could say they helped to build their own home?

So we worked out there on the prairie, beside our parents, digging up sod with shovels, scrapers, and other gardening and farming tools.

As I said before, it was tough work—made all the more difficult by the root network that branched out through every square inch of soil.

"How can plants have so many roots?" I asked my father, exasperatedly.

"Well, I don't know much about horticulture," said my father. "But I think these plants need so many roots because water's scarce out here. The roots draw every last bit of moisture out of the soil."

My mother added, "The roots anchor the plants against the prairie winds. We'll have to put down roots, too, or we'll blow away!"

By the time we went to sleep that night, inside our tent, I was more tired than I'd ever been before. It might take us days to build our house—or weeks—but we had seen that it was possible. Our little family of four, a group of Irish Americans who'd never seen any part of the country beyond the city streets of Philadelphia, was building a house on the prairie.

What a wonderful feeling of self-sufficiency! What a feeling of usefulness and capability! I slept soundly that night, and dreamed of sod.

The next day, we worked from sunrise to sunset. By nightfall, I was sick of sod. I hated its look, its smell, and its dirt and plant texture.

I wasn't alone in my feelings. I could tell that my mother, father, and sister were also tiring of the slow, repetitive, frustrating labor. But we carried on, without complaining. Like it or not, we were stuck here. We had nowhere else to go. And a house was a necessity. A tent would not make a good permanent residence, especially when the chilly winter winds arrived.

No, there was no question about it. A house, a sod house, was what we needed. We needed its shelter, its protection, and the warmth and comfort that it would provide.

So we soldiered on, day by day, week by week. We dug and cut and stacked sod. We piled up sod blocks, one atop the next.

And slowly, very slowly, we began to see the form of a house rise before us, on that desolate Nebraska plain.

Chapter Three

Two months later, I began to go to school again.

We had finally completed our soddy. There had been no shortage of backbreaking labor, but in the end, when we took a long, hard look at it, our house was definitely something to be proud of.

A little lumpy, sure. A bit on the rough and irregular side. It would certainly never win a "fancy house" contest sponsored by one of those ladies' journals that my mother had loved to read back in Philadelphia.

However, it served its purpose well. It was compact and sturdy and quite suited to our needs. It was a home, and in the end, that was what really mattered.

We had also begun to set up a rudimentary farm on our 160 acres. My mother had started to plant some basic subsistence crops in her garden. My father had erected a series of makeshift pens for the few animals we now owned: a couple of hogs, a dairy cow, a few stringy-looking chickens, and a horse.

We now owned a dog too. His name was Biscuit, and my sister adored him. It was Biscuit who seemed to miss me the most when I first began going to school. My parents said that when I left in the early morning, Biscuit would just sit and mope. It wasn't until I returned in the evening that he would perk up and bark.

The new school was very different from the one I'd attended in Philadelphia. That school had been an imposing red brick structure on a city block lined with buildings and teeming with activity.

My new school was off a dirt road, surrounded by miles of empty prairie.

In the Philadelphia school, you had to navigate a labyrinth of corridors to get from one classroom to the next.

In my new school, there were no corridors, and no other classrooms, either. There was just one room, holding about fifty students, ranging in age from five to eighteen. And there was just one teacher.

"Is this really it?" I asked one of my classmates, on my first day. "Is this the entire school?"

I was addressing a small blonde girl about my age, who was seated at a desk to my left.

She laughed and nodded, "Yes, this is the entire school. Just this room."

"How does it work?" I asked. "Do all the different grades do the same lessons together?"

"No," the girl laughed. "At the beginning of the day, the teacher gives each age group a reading and a writing assignment. Then, throughout the day, she meets with the students in each age group. While she's meeting with one group, the others work on their assignments."

"I see," I said, nodding. "So we don't learn the same stuff as the eighteen-year-olds, for example."

"Right," said the girl. "They have their lessons, and we have ours." She blushed and held out her hand. "I'm Maggie," she said.

I shook her hand and smiled. "I'm Timothy," I said.

"This school seemed strange to me too, at first," said Maggie with a faint Southern drawl. "We come from Eastbury, down in Georgia."

"We moved here from Philadelphia, a few months ago. But I couldn't come to school at first, because we had so much work to do," I told her.

"Did you build a soddy?" she asked.

"We sure did," I said. "Did you?"

"Everyone here does," she giggled.

"They seem so . . . flimsy," I whispered. "Do they ever fall down?"

Maggie giggled again. "No, but sometimes they leak when it rains."

I was about to ask more questions when a trim, young woman strode into the room. "Good morning, class!" she said in a crisp, loud voice.

"Good morning, Mrs. Apple," the students replied in unison.

Mrs. Apple sat behind her desk and slipped on a pair of spectacles. "We have a new student joining us today," she announced and fixed me with a firm but kindly look. "Timothy, would you please stand?"

Turning red, I obediently rose from my desk. I could feel 50 pairs of eyes swing toward me, and my heart started beating fast.

"This is Timothy O'Hare," Mrs. Apple told the class. "He and his family have just moved to Burgess from Philadelphia. He's ten years old, and he'll be your new classmate."

"Hello, Timothy," my classmates intoned, politely.

"Hello," I whispered back.

"You may be seated again, Timothy," said Mrs. Apple.

"Thank you, ma'am," I said, sinking back into my seat and wishing I were invisible.

That evening, Biscuit greeted me with enthusiasm, barking and jumping. I was almost as happy to see him as he was to see me.

It had been a long day in one room with so many older students. Some were the same age my mother was when she married my father! I felt keenly aware that I was still a ten-year-old. I knew I'd grow accustomed to the school, eventually. For the moment, however, it felt great to be out of that room. I felt like a newly released prisoner, freed from bondage, and wondering at the marvel of liberty.

"How was your first day of school?" my mother asked, cutting up butternut squash for dinner.

"It was okay," I said.

"And the teacher?" she asked. "Regina Apple is her name, I believe."

"Well, she seems to know a lot," I said.

"I should hope so," my mother laughed. "A teacher in a one-room schoolhouse better know a lot."

Chapter Four

With time, I did indeed come to like my new school, more and more.

I became good friends with Maggie, the girl I'd talked to on my first day. (In fact, eight years later, I went on to marry her. But that's another story.)

There were also a few boys in the class whom I quickly befriended. One of them, Michael O'Brien, was an Irish boy from back East—just like me!

I quickly found that the more friends I made, the easier it was to go to school each morning. Together, we formed a sort of close-knit mini-society within the larger student body.

We could stand firm, even against the menacing presence of any older students that we might encounter.

Actually, in all honesty, once you got to know them, the older students were rather friendly and not really menacing after all.

My days were fuller and longer than they had ever been in Philadelphia. I left the house at sunrise and seldom got home before 4:30 in the afternoon. Then I'd feed the animals and help my father until dinnertime. After dinner I'd do homework until bedtime. The next day, it would be more of the same.

It was overwhelming at first, but I saw that my parents worked just as hard without complaining, so I did the same.

Even my little sister did her part. Like me, Scarlet went to school, came home, and did chores. To my surprise, she didn't whine as she used to. The new Scarlet seemed to sense that we each had a job to do, if we were going to stay afloat in this new part of the world.

From sunrise to sunset, my father tended to our growing collection of livestock. He built a barn, a new pen for the hogs, and one for the goats. Frequently, he visited other homesteaders to learn more about agriculture and caring for animals.

My mother kept equally busy. She tended her garden, kept the house clean, and prepared three meals a day. It was a lot of work, but I can't remember ever hearing her complain about it.

Neither did my father, for that matter. They were tough people, my parents—tougher than I'd ever realized back in the city.

Our first winter in Nebraska was a difficult one. By November, it had become piercingly cold. The winter coats we'd brought from the East were next to useless against the Arctic winds that blew down from the north over the flat plains.

Inside our sod house, it wasn't too bad during the day. The sod walls trapped some heat inside. When the sun dipped below the horizon each evening, however, it got bitterly cold. At night, we huddled together under a ton of blankets.

Our lips became chapped, and the skin on our hands and feet grew dry and callused.

One November evening, our soddy was forced to stand up to the year's first heavy rainstorm. The house remained intact (thank goodness!), but a lot of mud and water dripped down from the roof.

To my surprise, half a dozen snakes also dropped down from the ceiling! How they had gotten up into the turf roofing was anyone's guess. They terrified my mother and sister as they slithered frantically across our floor, although we later found out that they had been of a fairly common (and nonpoisonous) variety.

Our house had stood up to the storm fairly well, but I now found myself nervously contemplating the effects that a heavy snowstorm might have upon our dwelling. These thoughts sometimes kept me up late at night.

"How do you like it here?" my classmate Michael O'Brien asked me abruptly one Saturday in early December.

We were gathered together, about five of us, in a field that belonged to old Mr. Partridge.

We had been playing tag for a good half hour and were now sprawled upon the ground.

"What do you mean?" I asked him.

"Nebraska," Michael said. "You've been here for half a year. What do you think of it?"

"I like it here," I began. "I mean, I'm lucky to have found such a good group of friends."

Michael blew a joking raspberry at me. "We know you like us, you big galoot," he grinned. "Why else would you waste so much time with us? But how do you like the place itself? The land, you know?"

"Well," I said, "all of our parents are homesteaders. We each own 160 acres of property. That's a lot, when you consider that, in Philadelphia, my family lived in a two-room apartment. You could probably fit it in our new property a hundred times over, or more."

All the kids nodded.

"But not everything here has been great," I continued. "The winter has been rough so far, for one thing."

The kids nodded knowingly.

"It gets so cold at night," I said. "The winds are so strong because there's all this open space."

More nods.

"One time, when it rained, snakes dropped down out of the roof!" I added. "Has that ever happened to any of you?"

Adam Millstone laughed. "I thought I'd go deaf—my sister Clara was screaming so loud!"

"So, do you like it here or not?" said Big Jimmy Dallup, the tallest, and stoutest, member of our gang.

"Oh, I like it," I explained. "But, it's a mix. Nothing is ever really all good or all bad, I guess."

"Every cloud has a silver lining," said Adam, nodding. "That's what my mom always says."

Chapter Five

Later that month, the snows arrived.

"Look!" Scarlet screeched one morning, rousing me from a fathoms-deep slumber. "Look at all the snow!"

Slowly, I pulled myself out of my nest of heavy blankets. "Wha'? Huh?" I said, not fully awake yet.

"Snow!" said Scarlet impatiently. "Snow, snow, snow! Lots of it! Tons! You've gotta look!"

Moving slowly, I somehow managed to rise from my bed. "You're waking me up just because it snowed?" I asked.

"It didn't just snow," huffed Scarlet. "It SNOWED! You have to see it!"

Finally, I moved to the window. A moment later, I was fully awake. "Wow! That's a lot of snow!" I shouted. "Mom and Dad, look!"

"Huh?" mumbled my father, his voice muffled under layers of blankets.

"It must be miles deep!" shrieked Scarlet, hugging herself with delight. "Miles!"

My father sat up slowly, then gave us a bleary-eyed grin. "You woke up your poor, exhausted father just because it snowed a little?" he asked us.

"Not a little!" Scarlet shouted. "Mountains! Mountains of snow!"

My mother elbowed my father gently. "Don't tease the children. It's clear they want you to go outside and play in the snow with them. Right, children?"

"Right!" we shouted.

He snorted as he put on his winter clothes, but as soon as we went out and dove into the mounds of freshly fallen snow, I could see that he was having as much fun as his children. Perhaps even more.

We played all morning, leaping and bounding, and rolling around in the fine white powder. We'd never seen snow like this before. In Philadelphia, the winter snows covered the roads and buildings, but there were no flat grasslands to fill up with a veritable empire of pure white snow.

It was wonderful. We threw volleys of snowballs and built an enormous snowman. Later, my mother bundled up and joined us. She pulled Scarlet on our toboggan, until they crashed into a fencepost. Neither was hurt. They just lay there together in the sifting, windblown snow, laughing until their sides hurt.

"Your mother isn't much of a sled-navigator," my father whispered to me, and I laughed too. It felt so good to have fun together. For the very first time, our small piece of Nebraska land began to feel a little bit more like home—a real home, that is.

I have many fond memories of the childhood years I spent growing up in Nebraska. But that first winter, with its prodigious snowfall and the wonderful winter games we played, provides me with some of the fondest of these.

I'm an old man now, well past my eightieth birthday. But when I look back on those snowy days, I can still feel the cleansing cold leaking through the fabric of my mittens. I can still taste the purity of a snowflake dissolving on the tip of my tongue. These images and impressions come back to me with a clarity, a vividness that is startling. It's as if I am transported back to my youth, and it feels like yesterday.

That winter was a key moment in my life. It marked the first time that I fell in love with my new home. Up to that point, it had been a barren, hostile landscape. But the winter and the snow changed all that.

Suddenly, everything seemed beautiful. The snow changed things, you see. It provided form where there had been none. It brought grace and balance where these qualities had been sorely lacking.

It showed me that my new home could be exciting, interesting, and even beautiful.

From that day on, Nebraska was my home. I came to love it as I had once loved the lively streets of Philadelphia. Perhaps even more.

And I am pleased to say that the bonds of friendship forged in childhood with Michael, Big Jimmy, Adam, and especially Maggie have endured for my entire adult life.

Now, I am not trying to pretend that life in Nebraska was easy. On the contrary, I cannot imagine an existence more beset by calamity and uncertainty. Hard winters, crop failure, illnesses, and financial ruination were facts of life. We faced each and every one of these hardships but somehow managed to fight them off, to stave off failure and make it through another day.

After five long years, the government agent came and inspected our 160 acres. He decided that we had, indeed, made a commendable number of improvements to the land, and he officially turned the property over to my mother and father.

I am proud to say that the land remains in my family to this very day.

Homesteaders of the Nineteenth Century

President Abraham Lincoln signed the Homestead Act in 1862, during the Civil War. The Act was designed to encourage Americans to move from the overcrowded East into the Western territories.

Under the provisions of the Act, citizens could claim 160 acres (one-quarter square mile) of surveyed government land in areas such as Nebraska and South Dakota. A homesteader, as such a person was called, was required to "improve" the land by planting crops and building a house. After five years, the land would legally become the homesteader's property.

Most homesteaders lived in sod houses built out of blocks of cut turf, held together by tough plant roots. These dwellings, called "soddies," were topped with a wooden roof covered with more sod. Soddies were cheap to build and provided good protection from the elements.

Homesteaders usually grew their own vegetables and ate a mix of livestock meat (beef and chicken) and wild game. They relied largely on buffalo chips and cow chips for fuel.